Look and Find®

KT-562-003

Disney PRINCESS

Wishes & Dreams

pi kids® publications international, ltd.

Tiana's dreams have come true! Welcome to Tiana's Palace, where the food is always hot and the music is smoking. Look for these signature dishes, made by Tiana herself.

Beignets

Gumbo

Braided sweet bread

Crawfish

Red beans and rice

Pecan pie

TIANA

*B*elle thought she was giving up everything by living in the castle with the Beast, but her life changed beyond her wildest dreams, and made all of her wishes come true! Can you find Belle's favorite stories in this room?

Romeo and Juliet

Thumbelina

Cinderella

Fairy Stories

Sleeping Beauty

The Princess and the Pea

Ariel collects human things from the ocean floor and wishes that one day, she could be part of the human world. Look for these human things Ariel has collected.

Hourglass

Candelabra

Fork

Box of thingamabobs

This painting

Pair of glasses

Snow White wishes that some day her prince will arrive—and her dreams will finally come true! Until then, she'll use a smile and a song to enjoy each day. Can you find these things that make Snow White smile?

Basket of ribbons

Pot of stew

Flowers

Baby bird

Clean dishes

Gooseberry pie

Rapunzel's wish has come true! She has escaped her tower and arrived in the heart of the nearby kingdom just in time for the lantern festival. Can you find people doing these things that she's been dreaming about?

Riding

Celebrating

Dancing

Splashing

Running

Flying

Sleeping Beauty used to dance with her prince once upon a dream, but now her dream has come true! Can you find her friends dancing at the ball with her?

Birds

Turtles

Rabbits

Squirrels

Chipmunks

Owls

Jasmine always dreamed about adventures outside of the palace walls. Aladdin and his magic carpet have made her dreams come true! Can you find these things that Jasmine has been wishing to see?

Fire-eater

Snake charmer

Human statue

Contortionist

Tightrope walker

Tiger tamer

Cinderella always said that a dream is a wish your heart makes — and her dreams of going to the ball and marrying the prince have come true! Can you find these things at Cinderella's wedding?

Violinist

Bouquet

Gus

Invitation

Bells

Cake

Tiana

Prince Naveen was able to make his dreams come true, just like Tiana. He's a jazz musician in New Orleans! Go back to Tiana's Palace to find these members of Naveen's jazz ensemble.

Belle

When Belle fell in love with the Beast, her dreams came true, and so did the dreams of her enchanted friends! Can you find human pictures of Belle's enchanted friends in the castle?

Cogsworth

Mrs. Potts

Beast

Puppy

Chip

Lumiere

Ariel

Go back to Ariel's grotto to find depictions of these things that Ariel can't wait to try on land.

Dancing

Carriage rides

Walking

Romance

Picnics

Beautiful dresses

Snow White

Just like Snow White, the Seven Dwarfs have their own wishes and dreams. Go back to the Dwarfs' cottage to find these things that they wish for.

Pocket watch

Dancing shoes

Roses

Kerchief

Accordion

Bedding

Snow White

Rapunzel

Rapunzel makes friends with thugs at the Snuggly Duckling that have hopes and dreams of their own. Can you find these thugs living out their dreams?

Sleeping Beauty

Flora and Merryweather wish that Sleeping Beauty's dress was pink…or blue! Can you find ball gowns at the palace in these colors?

Red

Purple

Yellow

Green

Orange

Brown

JASMINE

The Genie loves to grant wishes—if his master follows the rules! Can you find these people in Agraba who have had their wishes granted?

Cinderella

Cinderella's friends have wished for her happiness for so long! Can you find these household friends in Cinderella's wedding party?

Dreamers
Have
More Fun